The Book of Revelation: The History and Leg Book of the Bible

By Gustavo Vazquez-Lozano & Charles River Editors

Domenichino's *St. John the Evangelist*

About Charles River Editors

Charles River Editors is a boutique digital publishing company, specializing in bringing history back to life with educational and engaging books on a wide range of topics. Keep up to date with our new and free offerings with this 5 second sign up on our weekly mailing list, and visit Our Kindle Author Page to see other recently published Kindle titles.

We make these books for you and always want to know our readers' opinions, so we encourage you to leave reviews and look forward to publishing new and exciting titles each week.

Introduction

A Russian painting depicting Revelation 6:2

"And I saw, and behold a white horse: and he that sat on him had a bow; and a crown was given unto him: and he went forth conquering, and to conquer." – The Book of Revelation 6:2

About 2,000 years ago, a prophet named John wrote a book about his strange visions while he was in Patmos, a small Greek island in the Aegean Sea. This John, the Seer, the Revelator, was long believed to be one of Jesus's apostles, but recent historians have determined that he was a second-generation disciple. In fact, he was likely a political exile, writing for Christians under the threat of persecution by the Roman Empire, and his book, the Book of Revelation, was controversial, obscure, and rejected by many local churches as early as the 2nd century CE. Even after it managed to slip into the Bible as the last book of the canon, for years many doubted its authenticity, and others later branded it as the heretical hallucinations of a madman.

Despite those controversial origins, the Apocalypse or Revelation of John remains firmly embedded in the Bible as the final chapter of the great saga that opens with Genesis, the beginning of everything. As a bookend to Genesis, Revelation provides a narrative of the end times, the completion of history, and the end of the world. Genesis and Revelation thus constitute the Alpha and the Omega, a surprising expression that the Book of Revelation applies to the divinity. In the opening verses of the Book of Revelation, God says to John, "I am the Alpha and the Omega - the beginning and the end. I am the one who is, who always was, and who is still to come." John proclaims, "On the Lord's Day I was in the Spirit, and I heard behind me a loud voice like a trumpet, which said: `Write on a scroll what you see.'"

His esoteric narrative, impenetrable to most of his readers, is full of symbols, keys, and metaphors, abounds in strange visions and prophecies, monsters, natural catastrophes, and describes terrifying scenes that are typically described as apocalyptic. This fascinating book also features some of the most well-known religious concepts in the West, things that have provoked fear and fascination for centuries, including the four horsemen of the Apocalypse, the famous number of the Beast (666), the Antichrist (whom Revelation calls "the beast"), and the whore of Babylon.

Perhaps inevitably, the interpretation of the Book of Revelation has also generated significant controversy. Once it obtained its canonical status, meaning it was accepted by the whole Church as a divinely inspired text, countless generations immersed themselves in its verses in an effort to decode the visions of the prophet John. Theologians of many ages, and even recent Biblical scholars, have dissected the sentences and found clues regarding the work's authorship, context, and date of composition. One position is that Revelation is the literal truth of things to come, those who await the return of Christ in the clouds, commanding the Heavenly army, while others take a more spiritual interpretation. Still another position is that the book narrates events that were happening while John composed the tractate, and that it is a codified description, in terms which were understandable to the readers of its time, of the persecution of Christians under Emperor Nero or Emperor Domitian. A more intriguing proposition says that Revelation, in its primitive form, consisted of two or more shorter texts, and interestingly, that it originally formed a Jewish document that originally had nothing to do with Jesus.

In more modern times, some have characterized the Book of Revelation as a genocidal, bloody, warlike manifesto, but this is a naive interpretation because John the Seer wrote a message of radical change in the world, the rejection of an empire as the normality of history. In Jewish thought, the end of the world is not about despair, but about hope, and when Paul the Apostle wrote about the coming kingdom and the end of the age, he told his listeners and his readers,

"Encourage one another with these words." It was not something to be feared, but something to be expected with joy, and as the final book of the Bible, the last movement in a symphony of many authors composed over almost a thousand years, the task of Revelation was not easy. It required truly biblical proportions. For those like George Bernard Shaw, who viewed Revelation as nothing more than the hallucinations of a junkie, it must be noted that theologically and literarily, the great saga of angels and demons, kings and shepherds, cataclysms and miracles, divine revelations and great cosmic approaches deserved an epic closure, the final chapter that had to be as great as the beginning. And it did just that.

However, for John the Seer, his Apocalypse was a protest against the oppression of empires. John's visions imply that the reign of Rome was not the golden age of humanity and the culmination of civilization that the imperial propaganda wanted them to believe. Instead, the Roman Empire oversaw chaos, persecution, and injustice at the hands of beasts, and that while those on Earth were powerful, one day they would be judged. As Satan is thrown into a lake of fire, the tyrants and the powerful who oppress the weak will one day be dust and ruins. And interestingly, contrary to what most people think about the core message of Christianity, the final scene of the last book of the Bible is not about humans leaving the Earth, going up to a place called Heaven to live disembodied existences in eternal bliss. In fact, it is just the opposite. In the words of author Jonathan Kirsch, "Whether one sees in John's visions the destruction of the whole world or the dark tunnel that propels each one of us toward our own death, his final vision suggests that even after the worst we can imagine has happened, we may find the astonishing gift of new life."

The Book of Revelation: The History and Legacy of the Apocalyptic Final Book of the Bible examines what was written in Revelation, the authorship, and the history behind its placement in the Bible. Along with pictures depicting important people, places, and events, you will learn about Revelation like never before.

The Book of Revelation: The History and Legacy of the Apocalyptic Final Book of the Bible

The Apocalyptic Genre

The Book of Revelation appears under the title *Apocalypse of St. John* in most ancient manuscripts. Apocalypse is a Greek word that means uncovering, a disclosure of something important that was hitherto unknown, so revelation and apocalypse essentially mean the same thing.

The last book of the Bible belongs to a prophetical writing genre called apocalyptic literature, which was at its peak in the period known as Second Temple Judaism. Apocalyptic literature often involves revelations about the conclusion of history, the end of the present tyrannical world, or the establishment of the Messiah's kingdom, although this is not a rule. Usually, it provides a special secret knowledge or revelation from an initiate.

The genre's beginnings are located after the exile of the Jews to Babylon and was still very much alive in the time of the Essenes, John the Baptist, and Jesus and his apostles. Thus, when Christianity got its start, apocalyptic literature was at its peak, and today many scholars consider the gospels and many other writings of the New Testament to be apocalyptic literature - it is not necessarily about the end of the world, but about the conviction that God was about to intervene decisively and permanently in human history.

Both Second Temple Judaism and early Christianity produced several revelations besides John's, but only the Book of Daniel, written 300 years earlier, was included in the Old Testament. It contains clear points of contact with John's Book of Revelation, including that the prophet Daniel also presents himself as a seer, his visions involve beasts that come up from the sea, impossible for the imagination, and his visions find their climax at the end of time, when a celestial figure appears in the clouds to witness the resurrection of the dead and inaugurate a period of justice in which the righteous will shine like stars with God.

While the similarities with Revelation are clear, the author of *Daniel* did not invent the genre. A few years before the Book of Daniel reached its final form, the mysterious Book of Enoch, a collection of several manuscripts, had a section called Book of Watchers that discusses celestial beings and cosmic battles in Heaven and on Earth. Demons seduce women and create giants who populate the planet. The Book of Enoch is not in the Bible, but its worldview is present in parts of the New Testament and the literature of Second Temple Judaism, most prominently the Dead Sea Scrolls. Enoch's innovation was that he identified demons or Satan as a cosmic super adversary of God, an enemy from whom all bad things come. This is a far step from the traditional worldview of ancient Israel, where only God was in charge of all things - even bad things - that happen to humanity, such as oppression, tyranny, martyrdom, wars, plagues, and murder.

In addition to Enoch, other apocalypses composed before the birth of Christianity, or precisely in the period in which the first Christian texts were being compiled, include the Apocalypse of

Abraham, the Apocalypse of Adam, the Apocalypse of Elijah, and the Apocalypse of Moses, among others.

Although they differ in themes and characters, what distinguishes Jewish apocalyptic literature is the conviction that, in the face of flagrant injustice and suffering of his people, God will intervene in the end to fix the world - a great clean up - and bring the story to its climax.

The abundant apocalyptic production of the Jews is not found in the Bible, but its influence and ideas are found in many writings of the Old Testament and New Testament, and many religious scholars consider the Gospels as apocalyptic literature, especially Mark, Matthew, and Luke. Like his predecessors, Jesus as a prophet spoke about the end of the world, which would be preceded by cataclysms and misfortunes never before seen on Earth. Many readers may be unfamiliar with this image of Jesus as an end of the world prophet or the notion that the Gospels are apocalyptic literature, but in the Gospel of Mark, there is a chapter written in the style of the Book of Revelation known as the little apocalypse. It is a prophecy about the end of the world spoken of by Jesus himself, with cosmic catastrophes and angels abducting people.

In Chapter 13, after Jesus and his disciples complete the journey from Galilee to Jerusalem where they will meet their fate, they are in front of the magnificent temple and its buildings. One of the disciples said, "Teacher, look! What wonderful stones and what wonderful buildings!" Jesus responds with a bitter prediction, "Do you see all these great buildings? Not one stone here will be left on another; every one will be thrown down." The massive temple of Jerusalem represented the crowning achievement of civilization and was a symbol of eternity. Jesus's statement that one day there would not remain a single stone, but only dust, was as catastrophic as it was terrifying.

Sitting on the Mount of Olives, Jesus reveals to his closest disciples the secrets of the end times. First, he says, there will come a great social and family disruption in which humanity will suffer terribly, especially Christ's disciples. Rumors of war, famine, and earthquakes would be followed by the destruction of family and religious persecution: "You will be handed over to the local councils and flogged in the synagogues. On account of me, you will stand before governors and kings as witnesses to them. And the gospel must first be preached to all nations. Whenever you are arrested and brought to trial, do not worry beforehand about what to say. Just say whatever is given you at the time, for it is not you speaking, but the Holy Spirit. Brother will betray brother to death, and a father his child. Children will rebel against their parents and have them put to death."

According to Jesus, following the collapse of civilization will be a cosmic catastrophe causing the entire universe to show signs the time is approaching when the temple in Jerusalem is polluted by the "abomination that causes desecration," presumably a pagan idol in the sacred precinct. This event signals that God has departed from His dwelling place, followed by the appearance of false prophets claiming to be the Christ. When this happens, the universe itself will be shaken: "The sun will be darkened, and the moon will not give its light; the stars will fall from the sky, and the Heavenly bodies will be shaken." (Matthew 24:29).

Finally, says Jesus, God's envoy will appear to save from destruction those who remained faithful: "At that time people will see the Son of Man coming in clouds with great power and glory. And he will send his angels and gather his elect from the four winds, from the ends of the Earth to the ends of the Heavens." (Mark 13:26-27).

In Matthew 24:34, Jesus says that some standing with him would live to see all these things come to pass: "This generation shall not pass, till all these things be fulfilled."

Some scholars of the historical Jesus believe these apocalyptic elements were added to the gospels later, and that the preacher of Nazareth was not really waiting for the end, but either way, it is an established fact that the apocalyptic element was written about by early church leaders from the beginning. The letters of Saul of Tarsus, now known as Paul, the oldest extant documents that mention Jesus, are downright apocalyptic and contains links with Jesus's speech in Mark's little apocalypse. For the prophet of Tarsus, an agent of the devil had to appear before the end, and he would oppose Christ and his faithful and would have the power to create wonderful signs to deceive humans: "And then the lawless one will be revealed, whom the Lord Jesus will overthrow with the breath of his mouth and destroy by the splendor of his coming. The coming of the lawless one will be in accordance with how Satan works. He will use all sorts of displays of power through signs and wonders that serve the lie, and all the ways that wickedness deceives those who are perishing." (2 Thessalonians 2: 8-10).

Paul wrote that at the end of times, which could come at any moment, "The Lord himself, with a cry of command, with the archangel's call and with the sound of God's trumpet, will descend from Heaven, and the dead in Christ will rise first. Then we who are alive, who are left, will be caught up in the clouds together with them to meet the Lord in the air; and so we will be with the Lord forever. Therefore, encourage one another with these words." (1 Thessalonians 4: 16-17).

Even scholars who do not see Jesus as a prophet of the end of the world agree the early Church had an apocalyptic fervor and expected the Second Coming imminently. In this context, it is easy to see how the production of a document such as the Revelation of John fits perfectly in the New Testament. John of Patmos organized, extended, and developed themes barely hinted at in other documents included in the New Testament, and John's book answered the question that must have consumed the faithful's curiosity: what will the end be like if the book was composed, as most agree, amid religious persecution? Many readers and scholars have found it baffling that a Jewish Christian wrote the final book of the Bible, which is filled with strange visions, while contending with Roman authorities who regularly imposed cruel tortures on Christians, including being eaten by wild beasts before a roaring audience.

The oldest reference to Revelation is from Irenaeus, one of the Church fathers who lived in the

2nd century CE, who reported that the book "was seen" at the end of the reign of Emperor Domitian (95-96 CE). Victorinus of Pettau wrote that John the Apostle was exiled by Domitian to work in a mine on the island of Patmos, and it was on Patmos that he had the strange visions. This was an opinion shared by Saint Jerome.

An ancient bust of Domitian

St. John the Evangelist on Patmos by Hieronymous Bosch

However, the text of Revelation offers clues that it may have existed before Domitian's reign. Justin, Irenaeus, and Origen believed that the author of the Apocalypse was John the apostle of Jesus, but over time, historians who have analyzed the text have rejected that hypothesis definitively. The literary style, use of words, and theology of the Gospel of John and the Book of Revelation are so different that common authorship has been definitively ruled out. The only thing that all critics agree on is the place of Revelation's composition (present-day Turkey) and the approximate date (the last quarter of the 1st century CE).

Some parts of the book may actually be older. Most scholars agree the Book of Revelation in its current form resulted from a textual process that took several years and evolved from a simpler, shorter document. In other words, the text appears to have had several editors or redactional layers, which is not surprising given that the canonical gospels and many Old Testament books are also the results of the merge of several documents.

With the arrival of high Biblical analysis in the 19th century, some observed a lack of cohesion in the narrative, the existence of several doublets, and what they believed were unnecessary repetitions. Therefore, some proposed that similar to the first books of the Old Testament and some Gospels, the Book of Revelation was a compilation of several older texts that a Christian editor ended up stitching into a single tractate. In fact, some began to speculate that perhaps the final redactor had two or more Jewish apocalypses in front of him since the genre was booming at the time.

One German Biblical scholar in particular, Eberhard Vischer, proposed the Book of Revelation resulted from a long process. The first step was the union of Mark's little apocalypse and another Jewish text attributed to Cerinth, a Gnostic theologian who taught about a thousand-year reign of Christ from Jerusalem. According to Eusebius, Cerinthus "by means of revelations which he pretends were written by a great apostle, brings before us marvelous things which he falsely claims were shown him by angels; and he says that after the resurrection, the kingdom of Christ will be set up on Earth and that the flesh dwelling in Jerusalem will again be subject to desires and pleasures. And (...) that there is to be a period of a thousand years for marriage festivals."

Vischer

According to Vischer, these two texts were combined by Christians after the fall of Jerusalem during the First Jewish-Roman War. Based on this belief, the Revelation went through two expansions and redactions during two separate persecutions under the emperors Trajan and Hadrian. J. Weiss of Marburg advanced this theory, claiming the book was the result of combining a Christian apocalypse written during the persecution of Nero with a later Jewish text which consisted of a series of independent prophecies. James Tabor, famous for his book *The Jesus Dynasty*, believed that the Revelation was originally an entirely Jewish text that had nothing to do with Christ, and that the text speaks in code of events that occurred in Jerusalem *before* the destruction of the temple.

Josephine Massyngberde Ford proposed the fantastical theory that the oldest document of the current version of the book comes from the circle of John the Baptist, the super radical prophet who lived in the wilderness. Without a doubt, Ford's most extravagant claim is that the Revelation, or a good part of it, was written by John the Baptist himself, the predecessor prophet of Jesus, who according to the Gospels believed that the end times were coming and spoke of the "one who comes."

The reasons for believing that John the Baptist was the author were not entirely outlandish. Although John's preaching has been lost, fortunately the Gospels preserved a part of it, and in their works, the forerunner of Jesus appears in the Gospels as an apocalyptic prophet with a metaphoric language, threatening, full of images that remind readers of the intensity of Revelation. While preaching to the people, John says, "Who warned you to flee from the coming wrath? The ax is already at the root of the trees, and every tree that does not produce good fruit will be cut down and thrown into the fire." The Baptist then announces the future arrival of a divine envoy that will envelop the Earth with fire in a powerful act: "His winnowing fork is in his hand, and he will clear his threshing floor, gathering his wheat into the barn and burning up the chaff with unquenchable fire."

Despite the differing opinions of those who think that Revelation is the result of the union of several documents and those who believe an entirely Jewish text provided the origins of Revelation, both sides agree the first chapters addressed to the churches, as well as some parts at the end of the book, are the product of the last redactor. It is this last redactor and his context that offer clues as to the purpose and meaning of the book.

The Story

A medieval frontpiece for the Book of Revelation

The characters and concepts found in Revelation, such as the number of the beast and the kingdom of a thousand years, have had an extraordinary influence on the history of mankind. Its ideas have survived for centuries in commentaries on the Revelation, as well as art, religion, and even politics.

Revelation is addressed to seven Christian communities in Asia Minor, a region roughly contained in modern Turkey, and from the start it warns that the end is near. John the Revelator saw the beginning of a great tribulation in the persecution against Christians, and this would be followed by a cosmic battle between the forces of good and evil, which then concludes with the renewal of the Earth.

The book opens with the prophet John on the island of Patmos, which is only about 13 square miles, possibly walking along the beach and gazing at the dark sea. When John hears a voice behind him, he turns around and has a terrifying vision: the throne of God in Heaven. Next to the throne is a sacrificed lamb who tells him he is about to see the things to come in a short time – four horsemen go out riding, sowing calamities throughout the world: hunger, war, plague, and attacks by wild animals. John sees the souls of those who were killed for being faithful to God, asking for justice. John sees the same number of angels departing in the four directions, marking 144,000 people with a symbol to protect them from the impending calamities.

From the throne of God, John watches in terror as a star falls from Heaven to the world. The star opens an abyss from which giant, horrifying locusts emerge, and the devil's war against humanity begins. Next, John sees the Messiah's mother about to be attacked by a dragon, ready to devour her child as soon as it is born, but the woman escapes. The child is taken to Heaven, but to John's dismay, the war begins in Heaven between the archangel (or "super angel") Michael and the hosts of the dragon. The dragon is defeated, but the dragon escapes to bring desolation to the mother of the Messiah and her children on Earth. The dragon creates an alliance with two beasts who have the power to wage war against Christians. The first is a beast with seven heads and 10 horns (a symbol of Rome); and another whose name is equal to 666 (the emperor of Rome), who forces all inhabitants of Earth to worship the first beast, the empire. The first beast, writes Richard Bauckham, "represents the imperial power, the Roman Emperors as a political institution, and in particular their military might, on which the Roman empire was founded."

A medieval depiction of the seven-headed beast

William Blake's depiction of the dragon

As the angels release the wrath of God on the world, the demons gather the leaders of all nations for the great final battle in a place called Armageddon, a real territory that is located in the present state of Israel at the foot of Mount Carmel. The last angel sends an earthquake that destroys the city of Babylon, and John sees a symbol of the city: a whore riding a beast, drinking the blood of the martyrs, rejoicing. According to Bauckham, "In other words, Roman civilization, as a corrupting influence, rides on the back of Roman military power."

It is at this point that Jesus arrives. He is no longer the humble Galilean of the first coming seen in the Gospels, a helpless preacher who suffered a humiliating death before the power of Rome. Now Jesus returns as a warrior on a white horse, leading the Heavenly army. His robe has an inscription: King of King, Lord of Lords. He is more powerful than the beasts, and in the climactic moment of the book, Satan, his beasts, dragons, and followers are thrown into the fire and the righteous are resurrected to reign with Christ for a thousand years. But those righteous don't go to Heaven, and they are not caught up in the clouds to escape the Earth – instead, Heaven descends, and a new and resplendent Jerusalem settles on Mount Zion. Earth has started anew.

The Book of Revelation contains some of the most enduring ideas in the Bible. Even people who have never read the book, including non-religious people, have heard references to certain symbols that have become mainstays of contemporary culture.

The Second Coming refers to the day when Jesus Christ, temporarily absent from this world after the resurrection, returns to fulfill all divine promises. According to Revelation, this return will be evident, dramatic, and impossible for someone not to see it. Christ will not return to preach the gospel, because this time he will do justice by his own hand: "Now I saw Heaven opened, and behold, a white horse. And He who sat on him was called Faithful and True, and in righteousness He judges and makes war. His eyes were like a flame of fire, and on His head were many crowns. He had a name written that no one knew except Himself. He was clothed with a robe dipped in blood, and His name is called The Word of God." (Revelation 19:11-13).

The idea that Jesus will return once more did not originate in Revelation and was already present in the Gospels, where Jesus is reported as saying that the Son of Man would return within the lifetime of his followers.

The Rapture, as it is understood today, is not the evacuation of humanity to Heaven at the end of the world. Instead, it is the disappearance or kidnapping of a selection of special persons before the end times in order to spare them the suffering that is coming. This idea is probably a recent development, and it might not even be in the New Testament, but more recent Christians have cited a few verses from the Bible. Matthew 24:40-41 says, "Two men will be in the field; one will be taken and the other left. Two women will be grinding with a hand mill; one will be taken and the other left." Luke 17:34-35 says, "I tell you, on that night two people will be in one bed; one will be taken and the other left. Two women will be grinding grain together; one will be taken and the other left."

The New Testament describes Christ's reunion with the faithful when the end comes, and some are left behind, but not before the end of times. In Paul's epistles, documents that are older than the gospels, the idea that Jesus´s return was imminent is everywhere. Thus, when the first generation of Christians began to die out, there was confusion and disappointment because Jesus did not return, especially after the destruction of the Second Temple in Jerusalem at the hands of Rome in 70 CE. While some early writers changed the emphasis of the coming of the Kingdom to a more spiritual reality, in the Book of Revelation, John not only insists that Jesus will literally come down from the clouds, but also in a very different fashion: as a warrior at the head of a colossal army of angels, not to preach love for one another, but to annihilate with the sword the forces of Satan.

While the modern concept of the Rapture – the kidnapping of the elect before the Second Coming – is not in the Apocalypse, some have found a possible mention in the small and enigmatic paragraph in Revelation 3:10-11, although this reading seems forced. "Since you have kept my command to endure patiently, I will also keep you from the hour of trial that is going to come on the whole world to test the inhabitants of the Earth. I am coming soon."

The battle of Armageddon is mentioned in the Apocalypse as the site of the final confrontation between the cosmic forces of evil and the armies of Christ. The word Armageddon, which has come to mean a great conflict, appears only once in the Bible, and it means "on the mountain of Megiddo." Revelation 16:16 says, "Then they gathered the kings together to the place that in Hebrew is called Armageddon."

Armageddon was well-known at the time to the locals as an old battle site, best remembered for being the place where Pharaoh Necho killed the king of Israel, Josiah. Since there are no mountains in Megiddo, the term has proved problematic for exegetes, but Vischer proposed a creative solution: he understood the word Armageddon as a place mentioned in the Book of Enoch, where the demons gather on a mountain for their final assault on the daughters of men. Behind the reference to Armageddon, it is suggested, lies an ancient myth of demons gathering on a mountain who are then destroyed by the gods.

One of Revelation's most memorable aspects is the number of the beast: "It (the beast) also forced all people, great and small, rich and poor, free and slave, to receive a mark on their right hands or on their foreheads, so that they could not buy or sell unless they had the mark, which is the name of the beast or the number of its name. This calls for wisdom. Let the person who has insight calculate the number of the beast, for it is the number of a man. That number is 666."

The number 666 was likely used by John as a key to designate the beast that comes out of the sea as the agent of Satan. It is an alphanumeric key to avoid a real name, and thus possibly avoid going to prison or being crucified, but it has also allowed people to speculate over it ever since. Each generation has had its candidates, from Muhammad to Hitler, but when describing the great tribulations that the power of Satan was unleashing, it is most likely that John was not predicting the future. If anything, he was probably talking about events that were unfolding before his eyes, and the beast was a character from his own time.

Many Biblical scholars believe that 666 most likely refers to Emperor Nero, who was the first to unleash a policy of annihilation against Christians with a cruelty and viciousness that even now seems excessive. In 64 CE, the Great Fire of Rome devastated the Eternal City, and despite popular belief, it is extremely unlikely that Nero caused the fire. Though legend – and some ancient historians – claim that Nero wanted to create space for the palace he eventually erected over much of the ruins, the fabled Domus Aurea ("Golden House"), there are several facts that contradict this theory. First, Tacitus, who was actually alive at the time of Nero's reign, suggests that he was not in Rome at all, but in nearby Antium. Secondly, astronomers have established that the night of July 18 was two days shy of a full moon, which seems to make arson unlikely since arsonists would hardly want to pick a night during which they were more likely to be seen. Moreover, the fire itself actually damaged a significant part of the Domus Transitoria, Nero's palace prior to the Domus Aurea, and though the fire that he planned may have gotten out of control, it is unlikely that he would have wanted – or even risked – setting his own palace alight.

It is most likely that the fire was an accident, likely caused by flammable materials near the Circus Maximus. Indeed, blazes of such kind were common until the 19th century in overcrowded cities with wooden houses closely packed together, lit and heated by open flames, and with no organized official fire brigades. In fact, Rome would suffer two more major fires in the next 15 years.

Regardless of its origins, the fire was a disaster for Rome. Though casualties are unknown, it destroyed scores, if not hundreds, of private residences, commercial premises, and public buildings. According to Tacitus, Nero quickly hurried back from Antium when news reached him of the fire and opened the doors of his palace to common people dispossessed by the flames. Tacitus claim Nero also spent days, sometimes without his bodyguards, combing the smoking ruins for victims and partially funding the relief effort out of his own private fortune. Though this is partially at odds with Nero's perceived character, his populist generosity to the lower classes, which was a hallmark of his reign, was in keeping with his previous legislation and sounds like it could have a kernel of truth.

An ancient bust of Nero

Either way, the Great Fire of Rome permanently tarnished Nero's reign, and it ultimately helped bring about the downfall that ended with the Roman emperor committing suicide just a few years later in 68. Before that, however, he sought to exonerate himself in the eyes of his people by blaming someone else, and conveniently, Christians were the perfect scapegoats. Christianity was still a secretive sect that could boast only small numbers, but it was fast growing in popularity and was thus viewed with suspicion and even hatred by the Roman Empire, much the same way Jews were. The main reason for this dislike was simple - the other pagan polytheistic traditions which flourished side by side throughout the Roman Empire might advocate the superiority of their own particular gods, but unlike the Christians, they would not deny the existence of others. Christians believed that theirs was the only true God and were not afraid to say it. That made them quite unpopular, as did the fact that the Christian religion had very clearly sprung up out of Judaism and hailed from the same region as the Jews.

Nero capitalized on the unpopularity of Christians by accusing them of being responsible for the blaze, though it does not appear as though any motive was ever ascribed to them. Several were seized and tortured, after which they confessed. It's actually unclear whether these people confessed to being Christians or to the arson itself, but most sources agreed that these people confessed as a result of torture. In any event, dozens of Christians were killed in response to the Great Fire, making them some of Christianity's first martyrs. The first institutionalized persecution of the Christians in the history of the Roman Empire had begun, and it would certainly not be the last.

Henryk Siemiradzki's *Christian Dirce*, which depicts a Christian woman being martyred

For most of history, Nero was believed to be responsible for killing hundreds of Christians in the cruelest ways possible, and even today, he is considered perhaps the worst persecutor of

Christians among the Roman emperors. That said, the accusations against him have been questioned in recent years. It's an indisputable fact that Nero had Christians killed, but scholars are unsure just how many Christian martyrs suffered under his reign. St. Paul and St. Peter wrote letters that sent greetings to certain Christians in Rome, and some scholars have asserted that since these letters contain only a few names, they are evidence that there were only a handful of Christians in Rome during the time of Nero.

However, there are two problems with this theory. First, since Christianity was quickly expanding at the time, there would have been no way for Paul, Peter or anyone else to keep up with the names of every Christian living in Rome. In fact, even if they had a list of names, they would not necessarily have sent greetings o each specific individual. Instead, they would likely have named those whom they knew most personally. Likewise, during a time of persecution when people's lives were threatened, they were not likely to make a long list of names in their letters lest the documents fall into the wrongs hands.

No matter how many Christians Nero actually put to death, the cruel ways in which he went about executing them were reason enough to make him notorious. Tacitus described the persecution, and in doing so, he became one of the earliest historians to make a historical reference to Jesus: "But all-human efforts, all the lavish gifts of the emperor, and the propitiations of the gods, did not banish the sinister belief that the conflagration was the result of an order. Consequently, to get rid of the report, Nero fastened the guilt and inflicted the most exquisite tortures on a class hated for their abominations, called Christians by the populace. Christus, from whom the name had its origin, suffered the extreme penalty during the reign of Tiberius at the hands of one of our procurators, Pontius Pilatus, and a most mischievous superstition, thus checked for the moment, again broke out not only in Judaea, the first source of the evil, but even in Rome, where all things hideous and shameful from every part of the world find their centre and become popular. Accordingly, an arrest was first made of all who pleaded guilty; then, upon their information, an immense multitude was convicted, not so much of the crime of firing the city, as of hatred against mankind. Mockery of all sorts was added to their deaths. Covered with the skins of beasts, they were torn by dogs and perished, or were nailed to crosses, or were doomed to the flames and burnt, to serve as a nightly illumination, when daylight had expired. Nero offered his gardens for the spectacle, and was exhibiting a show in the circus, while he mingled with the people in the dress of a charioteer or stood aloft on a car. Hence, even for criminals who deserved extreme and exemplary punishment, there arose a feeling of compassion; for it was not, as it seemed, for the public good, but to glut one man's cruelty, that they were being destroyed."

As Tacitus's account suggests, though most Romans were not Christians, the empire was known for a certain limited level of religious tolerance, even in the provinces they conquered. Thus, the idea that Nero was also burning otherwise loyal Roman citizen who just happened to be followers of a Jewish carpenter disturbed many in the city, even if they were distrustful of the religion itself.

In a sense, it's ironic that Nero's attempt to scapegoat Christians and snuff out their religion in Rome only ensured that he would forever be tied to the history of Christianity. As a result, his legacy remains so intertwined with the persecution of Christians that he is perhaps more notorious for that than anything else.

Even after Nero committed suicide, throughout the remainder of the 1st century, the legend ran that Nero would live again or that he had not really died, and that he would return from the East with a great army to destroy Rome. The legend that Nero would return persisted all the way into the 4th century, which may explain why Revelation describes a beast that once was, that does not exist in its present, and that will rise again from the abyss: "The beast, which you saw, once was, now is not, and yet will come up out of the Abyss." A reference to Nero's death and rumors of resurrection can be found also in Revelation 13:3: "One of the heads of the beast seemed to have had a fatal wound, but the fatal wound had been healed. The whole world was filled with wonder and followed the beast. "

In the middle of the book, John sees an angel chain the dragon for a thousand years, the length of Christ's new reign. According to Revelation, "And I saw the souls of those who had been beheaded because of their testimony about Jesus and because of the word of God. They had not worshiped the beast or its image and had not received its mark on their foreheads or their hands. They came to life and reigned with Christ a thousand years. "

All cultures believe that one day there will be a destructive transformation in history, after which there will be a lengthy utopia, and the predominant notion in the Western world comes from the Book of Revelation, which announces that after the resurrection of the martyrs, they will live and reign with Christ during a thousand-year messianic rule. (Revelation 20: 4-6). The idea of this thousand-year kingdom or empire has left its mark on human history and moved great masses, including nations. Two examples are the hysteria unleashed in Europe before the approach of the year 1000, and more recently Hitler's Third Reich, which he vowed would last a thousand years.

In Revelation 12, another great cosmic symbol appears: the woman who is heavily pregnant and is threatened by a monster. One of the most striking symbols of Revelation is most likely a third narrative of Jesus's birth retold in symbolic terms, in the style of this author: "A great sign appeared in Heaven: a woman clothed with the sun, with the moon under her feet and a crown of twelve stars on her head. She was pregnant and cried out in pain as she was about to give birth. Then another sign appeared in Heaven: an enormous red dragon with seven heads and ten horns and seven crowns on its heads. Its tail swept a third of the stars out of the sky and flung them to the Earth. The dragon stood in front of the woman who was about to give birth, so that it might devour her child the moment he was born. She gave birth to a son, a male child, who 'will rule all the nations with an iron scepter.' And her child was snatched up to God and to his throne. The woman fled into the wilderness to a place prepared for her by God." (Revelation 12:1-6).

A medieval depiction of the woman and the beast

If true, then the Bible contains not only the birth narratives of Matthew and Luke, but also the one in Revelation. The woman who is about to give birth to the Messiah is Mary, the mother of Jesus. John retells the well-known Matthean narrative of Jesus's birth, which vividly depicts the bestial Herod (in the service of Rome) planning to assassinate the child as soon as Herod can find Jesus's location. However, thanks to the warning of the Three Magi, the mother flees to Egypt and crosses the desert until the designated time to return to Judea is fulfilled.

The final image of the Apocalypse, and of all the Bible for that matter, is the descent of Heaven and God's rule to the Earth, not the other way around. A renewed Earth and a new Heaven appear in the prophet's vision. The sea, which was a symbol of chaos and the forces of the abyss, had disappeared. After contemplating the new Earth and the new Heaven, an angel leads John to witness the descent of a huge city, which the prophet describes in words reminiscent of the distant Earthly paradise at the beginning of the Bible, in Genesis: "Then I saw 'a new Heaven and a new Earth,' for the first Heaven and the first Earth had passed away, and there was no longer any sea. I saw the Holy City, the new Jerusalem, coming down out of Heaven from God, prepared as a bride beautifully dressed for her husband."

Unlike the Heavenly paradise, where the Creator seems to be only a voice from above, now human beings can see God because the throne is in the middle of the garden. According to Revelation 22:1-2, "The angel showed me the river of the water of life, as clear as crystal, flowing from the throne of God and of the Lamb down the middle of the great street of the city. On each side of the river stood the tree of life."

In this way, the circle is closed, and the lost paradise is recovered. For this reason, the Book of Revelation, which entered the canon through the last crack that was already closing, constitutes an appropriate ending to the collection of works.

The Revelation after John

The apocalyptic, millennial, vindictive character, and extravagant collection of visions of Revelation provoked controversy among the first Church fathers. Thus, it should come as little surprise that Revelation's inclusion in the New Testament canon was a long and tortuous process, and it barely made it. The Church fathers Irenaeus, Tertullian, Hippolytus, Origen, and Clement of Alexandria mentioned it in their writings and accepted it as inspired Scripture, while Clement of Alexandria also accepted the Apocalypse of Peter, which did not make it into the canon.

Hippolytus, who is possibly the author of the Muratorian canon, the oldest surviving list of New Testament books, offered up a passionate defense of John's book. Dionysus, a bishop of Alexandria, Egypt, wrote in the 3rd century that some in the Church rejected it because it seemed senseless and illogical, but Dionysius accepted it because he realized that many Christians had it in high regard. Dionysius did so despite the fact he did not believe that the author of John's Gospel and the Revelation were the same person, and he also confessed that the enigmatic book exceeded his capacity for understanding: "For, though I do not understand it I suspect that some deeper sense is enveloped in the words, and these I do not measure and judge by my private reason; but allowing more through faith, I have regarded them as too lofty to be comprehended by me, and those things which I do not understand, I do not reject."

Dionysius's modest position was the exception. All early commentators on the Church were embroiled in controversy regarding its interpretation, especially the thousand-year reign of Christ and what exactly that millennium would look like. The idea that Revelation spoke literally of a thousand-year rule of the Messiah divided the early Church. Tertullian, a 2nd century Christian writer, wrote during the persecution that John's Revelation, with all its terrible imagery, was actually God's stance against an oppressive empire that was temporarily in charge of the world (Rome), and that the prophet John declared the freedom of Christians against this demonic power. According to Tertullian, John's work defiantly proclaimed, "Never will I call the emperor` god´. I am willing to call him 'lord' in the ordinary sense of the term, but my relationship to him is one of freedom." To him, that was the true spirit of the book.

For some, the Book of Revelation was a prophecy of what would happen in the future after a period of abundance marked by too much eating, drinking, marrying, and having children. This interpretation was advocated by Justin Martyr and Ireneus, but others criticized this vision as too sensual. Another interpretation held that the defeat of Satan and the beginning of the thousand-year reign had already occurred with the crucifixion and resurrection of Jesus and that the thousand years would correspond to the life of the Church.

In the 4th century, Eusebius, the first great Church historian, included the Revelation of John, the Apocalypse of Peter, the Didache, and the Acts of Paul in his collection of doubtful books, attesting to their use in some quarters of Christendom and their rejection in other churches. Regarding Revelation specifically, Eusebius cited a learned churchman called Gaius, who lived in Rome and accused a man named Cerinthus of having made a forgery, an opinion that Epiphanius repeated. By that time, however, the two authors were already too far removed from the composition of the Revelation to have reliable sources.

Throughout the first several centuries, the book was almost unknown in the Eastern Church. As late as the 7th century, the Council of Toledo in Spain noted that many churches refused to read it and imposed sanctions for those who would not include it in the liturgy. Today, the Orthodox Church accepts it as a canonical book, but the Orthodox Church has excluded it from liturgical celebrations. In the Catholic liturgy, it is read only once or twice a year.

An Orthodox icon depicting scenes from Revelation

The Book of Revelation entered the canon definitively in the 5th century, while the Apocalypse of Peter, which speaks of the punishments of the damned in Hell, was left out. Athanasius, the first person to identify the 27 books of the New Testament, accepted the Apocalypse of John as inspired Scripture, and despite almost three centuries of debates, it managed to sneak in, occupying the last place of the Christian Bible and the New Testament. Its inclusion makes sense when one considers that the collection opens with Genesis, an account of the creation of the world, and the Revelation closes with the end of human history.

Even after Revelation was included in the canon, the debate whether the Revelation spoke of past events, spiritual realities, or things that would come in the future as described in its verses continued within the Church. The interpretation of Saint Augustine, born in North Africa, was the one that finally prevailed. Known as the Doctor of Grace, Saint Augustine did not agree with the millennialism of his contemporaries - instead, he believed the Book of Revelation spoke of spiritual truths and that the millennium had already begun with the Church's establishment. Contrary to his contemporaries' expectations, Augustine developed an interpretation of sacred history practically ignorant of time. For Augustine, humanity could not know anything about the time and mode of the end of the world, much less the details and the signs of its proximity, or how to determine who was to be saved and who was to be damned. Only until the return of Christ would the good and the evil be separated, so those who said they could "read" historical events as omens of the end were wrong. Thus, when Rome was sacked in 410 by Alaric's forces and terrified Christians took it as a symbol of the end, Augustine was able to say that the true City of God was spiritual, and it was there that the Most High really reigned, not in Rome.

The Middle Ages

For the next 800 years, Saint Augustine's interpretation would dominate ecclesiastical commentaries and theological treatises on Revelation, and the so-called "allegorical millennialism" became the official doctrine of the Church. However, as the Middle Ages advanced, and with it the corruption of the Church and its departure from its original spirit, many began to see that the New Testament not only preached literal truths but possibly spoke of the corruption of the religious authorities. Millennialism, especially the idea that a thousand-year cycle would soon begin after being preceded by fantastic signs, spread across medieval Europe, and people were constantly torturing themselves with prophecies, superstitions, and omens. The expectation was exacerbated by the approach of the year 1000.

Rodolfus Glaber, a French monk and historian, was the era's best source on the turn of the millennium in Europe. In his work *Miracles of Saint-Benoit,* Glaber wrote that around the year 1000, Europe was burning with end of the world expectations and the second coming of Christ due to "the prophecy of the apostle." Seven years before that fateful year, Mount Vesuvius threw flames and rocks like never before seen in that generation, and the projectiles fell several miles away from the crater, rendering the surroundings uninhabitable. Other events people took as signs of the impending apocalypse were "a great conflagration in Rome," pestilence in several cities in Italy and France, and a fire in the seat of papal power, St. Peter's Basilica, which consumed part of the church. According to the monk, when people saw things like this, they shouted, hugged each other, and asked for confession en masse.

With a new millennium approaching, people began to rebuild or renovate churches in Italy and France, even though they did not need repairs, and the relics of many saints, which had been kept hidden for centuries, were displayed to the public to "decorate the new era." According to the historian, the sight of the relics brought much comfort to the people.

In the year 1009, the millennial fervor was still alive and would continue until the year 1033, which marked a thousand years since Jesus's crucifixion. In 1009, the Caliph of Jerusalem ordered the destruction of all churches, and the Jews in Europe suffered persecutions for this cause, apparently as part of the destruction of the enemies of Christianity that should take place at the end of times. Glaber noted, "Some were slain with the sword or cut off by manifold kinds of death, and some even slew themselves in diverse fashions; so that, after this well-deserved vengeance had been wreaked, scarce any were found in the Roman world."

As the year 1033 approached, Glaber wrote that large crowds made a pilgrimage to Jerusalem to the tomb of Jesus, "as no man could before have expected." From kings to humble women, when he asked the crowds why they were making the pilgrimage, they "answered with some caution that it portended no other than advent of that reprobate Antichrist."

The most important apocalyptic thinker of the Middle Ages was a layman named Joachim of Fiore, who was born in Calabria, Italy. During a visit to Jerusalem, Fiore had a mystical experience that completely changed his life. A poet and an artist, Joachim became a monk and retired to the mountains to live a contemplative life, not much differently than John of Patmos, and he became obsessed with the Book of Revelation. He was increasingly frustrated by its difficult reading until he believed he had an epiphany of his own that opened his understanding. Based on his readings of Revelation, Fiore developed a philosophy of history divided in three stages: the era of the Father, corresponding to the epoch before the coming of Christ; the era of the Son, which he was living in; and the Era of the Spirit, a future millennial time, which he thought was imminent. But according to Fiore, the world must first pass through the coming of the Antichrist and a great tribulation. For Fiore, the third era would be characterized by a more spiritual Church - less materialistic - and a deeper spiritual awareness. Instead of a Second Coming of Christ, the Holy Spirit would create a new breed of men, a new epoch of peace would begin, Jews and Christians would reunite, and the Church clergy would become obsolete. He prophesied the advent of new orders of spiritual men and developed a ground plan for the New Jerusalem. The British historian Norman Cohn opined that Fiore anticipated Marxism, describing the last stage of humankind, the age of the Spirit, as primitive communism, a class-free society and the disappearance of the state.

A Renaissance depiction of Fiore

Although Fiore's writings were approved and admired in his lifetime, after his death they were attacked and feared by men of power within the Church who considered his ideas too dangerous. To this day, the debate continues whether Joachim of Fiore was a heretic or a saint, but his reading of Revelation and theory of the three eras influenced the appearance of more spiritual orders like the Franciscan and Dominican mendicant orders, and it emboldened others to criticize the power of the Church.

The Modern Era

The Protestant Reformation and the great division of the Roman Catholic Church led to many revisiting the Book of Revelation and reinterpreting its prophecies. For Marin Luther, an obscure monk who suddenly saw himself as the leader of the schism, it was natural to interpret his times in apocalyptic terms. Initially, he rejected the Book of Revelation, but he soon realized that he could rely on it to explain what was happening. In his vision, Luther was fighting for purity inside Christianity, and the pope in the Vatican was nothing less than the beast of Revelation. As such, Luther thought the book belonged in the canon but separated, along with the other books in a "disputed" section. Luther explained, "My spirit cannot accommodate itself to this book. For me this is reason not to think highly of it: Christ is neither taught nor known in it." Lucas Cranach the Elder, a friend of the monk who fervently embraced the Protestant cause, made some famous pictures of the whore of the Book of Revelation wearing the papal tiara, which he painted for Luther's New Testament.

Lucas Cranach's illustration

Luther

Ulrich Zwingli could not accept Revelation because its abundant use of angels encouraged what he considered an immature, pious mysticism, and its liturgical format was too close to the Catholic mass. Zwingli asserted, "With the Apocalypse, we have no concern, for it is not a biblical book...I can, if I so will, reject its testimonies." John Calvin did not voice much of an opinion on Revelation – although he occasionally quoted it, his commentaries excluded it.

The European colonization of the New World brought Revelation to the forefront in the minds of many colonizers who moved overseas. The concepts of the New Jerusalem, new Heaven, and new Earth were revived by Puritan preachers in the American colonies who were convinced - or tried to convince their listeners - that by fleeing the corrupt churches of Europe, they were inaugurating the new messianic era described by John in Revelation. They never considered that to achieve this, they had to massacre the native peoples of America. "Christ by a wonderful Providence hath dispossessed Satan, who reigned securely in these Ends of the Earth, for Ages the Lord knoweth how many," said another Puritan preacher a century later when he set foot in the colonies, "and here the Lord has caused as it were New Jerusalem to come down from Heaven."

On countless occasions, artists have been inspired by the scenes described in Revelation and produced superb works, including the paintings of Hieronymoush Bosch and Michelangelo, as well as the engravings of Albrecht Dürer and the haunting illustrations of Gustave Doré. In the mid-18th century, one of the best-known choral pieces in the West premiered – the oratorio called "Messiah," by George Frideric Handel, a composition that reaches a wonderful climax at the end of part II with the choir of Hallelujahs. There, angelic voices in crescendo announce the eschatological victory of Christ using several lines from the Book of Revelation. The beautiful choirs, frequently used for the most impressive Christmas performances, do not actually announce the birth of Jesus in Bethlehem. The triumphant hallelujahs and the reiterations "King of Kings, Lord of Lords" correspond to the terrifying scene of Jesus, king and warrior, riding his white horse, dressed in a robe dipped in blood, sowing destruction among his enemies, while a great earthquake wipes out civilization.

Michelangelo's *The Last Judgment*

In the 20th century, the insightful British historian Norman Cohn emphasized the resemblance between the apocalyptic beliefs of the Middle Ages and the great statist revolutions and movements of his century, which were in turn fueled by beliefs associated with medieval apocalyptic movements. As he put it, "In situations of mass disorientation and anxiety, traditional beliefs about a future golden age or messianic kingdom came to serve as vehicles for social aspirations and animosities."

In conjunction with that, Cohn observed that in the 20th century, the secular language had adopted apocalyptic categories and a millennial discourse. Although this is not obvious at first glance, he said, "It is the simple truth that, stripped of their original supernatural sanction, revolutionary millenarianism and mystical anarchism are with us still." This need to purify the Earth through the eradication of a certain group of people who are seen as representatives of evil is still present in the world under different disguises, but its roots are the same: the old apocalyptic thinking of the Middle East, fueled by the Book of Revelation. According to Cohn, when these apocalyptic forces awaken in moments of crisis, famine, war, or national threat, "this underworld becomes a political power and changes the course of history."

Cohn believed the expectations of a great tribulation followed by a golden period managed to survive throughout the centuries, changing borders and political systems, and moving from the realm of religion to the public domain without losing their strength or ability to incite those who suffer. In this sense, Cohn suggested that cult of personality like Hitler and Stalin "appealed to the deep, biblically inspired belief that, after intense struggle, history would end, and an elect of believers would inherit paradise."

In this same sense, books like *The Protocols of the Elders of Zion*, a fabricated antisemitic work that had enormous influence on Hitler and other German leaders, were fueled by old ideas of the Jews as an evil race and the children of the devil. The combination of this notion and a racist ideology would produce the Holocaust, and the belief that the Earth needed to be saved by the "world of good, of light, incarnated in blond, blue-eyed people marching under the sun-god's symbol, the swastika." That Hitler was thinking in apocalyptic terms is clear from his conviction to form a thousand-year Third Reich, a new and terrible form of millennialism.

Especially after the horrors of World War II and the Holocaust, many nations with Christian presidents supported the proposal to create a homeland for the Jews in Palestine. However, support for the creation of Israel may have been in part due to the apocalyptic idea that the Jews should be in their homeland, with a functioning temple, for the end times to begin. According to Revelation, "When the angel sounds the seventh trumpet, God's temple in Heaven was opened, and within his temple was seen the ark of his covenant. And there came flashes of lightning, rumblings, peals of thunder, an earthquake, and a severe hailstorm." These words lead readers to assume that a new temple will be functioning in Mount Zion, and many Christian and evangelical fundamentalists saw the creation of the new state of Israel in 1948 and the rumors about the construction of a third and final temple in Jerusalem as apocalyptic signs.

If these ideas seem too outlandish, it is even more surprising to know that, as Cohn explained, the concept of the Middle East as a necessary region for the Second Coming of Christ influences current international politics. While not all international policy makers who are Christians have this view of the apocalypse, Christian fundamentalists are generally pre-millenarians who believe in the Rapture, and that humans can contribute to the faster arrival of the kingdom. "Among the many approaches to interpretation of prophecy, there are two distinct camps," writes Robert Leonhard of Johns Hopkins University. "On the one side is premillennialism that predicts a future return of Christ, who intervenes violently to establish his kingdom on Earth. On the other side is post-millennialism, which deprecates the idea that Christ will someday return and destroy the establishment, but instead believes that the role of the Church is to spread Christ's love and improve the world until he returns for the final judgment. These two competing ideas about Christian prophecy have enduring influence on policy in the Western world."

In 1970, *The Late Great Planet Earth* was published by Hal Lindsey, an evangelical pastor, and it would become the best-selling nonfiction book of the 1970s. As many others before him, Lindsey predicted that the events of Revelation would take place in his generation and that the Antichrist had been born and was beginning to act on Earth. The book noted the frequency of earthquakes, famines, and wars, and predicted Europe would become a great political union that would form the new Roman Empire, ruled by the Antichrist. The Soviet Union would invade Israel, and these events would precipitate the end. Lindsey suggested these events would all take place in the 1980s.

Doomsday Cults

"Believers and churches that experience the success of Christianity- either in the Church's beneficent influence in the world or its integration with political authority-tend to view the kingdom prophecies as present realities. Those who experience persecution or suppression of Christianity tend to look for a future kingdom that supplants the present condition." - Robert Leonhard, *Visions of Apocalypse.*

Religious fundamentalism is a product of modernity. Understood as a defensive reaction to the decline of religious thought and authority, in the face of a scientific mindset and naturalism, religious fundamentalism is a relatively new phenomenon. The greatest scientific advances in humanity did not bring about the disappearance of religion as many thought, but it did erode the power of large institutions such as the main Christian churches.

At the same time, humanity found new ways to express its religious convictions, sometimes even more acutely in the case of doomsday cults. In the late 19th century and early 20th century, fundamentalism in the United States began as a stream emanating from Princeton Theological Seminary in response to modernism and new ways of interpreting the Bible. At the beginning of the 19th century, an Adventist movement in the United States proclaimed the Second Coming of Christ. Specific dates were offered, and around this time, Charles Taze Rusell founded the Jehovah's Witnesses, a Christian sect that relies on the Book of Revelation as the basis of its preaching and its millennial vision of history.

At the end of the 19th century, one of the major evangelical centers of the United States preached his revivalist ideals and started a wave of evangelism that would last well into the 20th century. Dwight Moody, an American evangelist who founded the Moody Church, deplored the new scholarly readings of the Bible, the theory of evolution, and preached a literal Second Coming of Christ happening soon.

Moody

With the arrival of the 20th century, there were energetic reactions from the apocalyptic cults, and many of them found in Revelation their reason for existing and their expectations of the imminent end of the world. In some cases, these cults tried to help bring it about: if the end of the world didn't come, they wanted to do something about it.

The most shocking case was that of the Peoples Temple of Indiana, under the charismatic leadership of Jim Jones, who moved his congregation to Guyana in 1978 and ordered the mass suicide of more than 900 members. The images of the Jonestown commune in Guyana, filmed from a helicopter, showed viewers hundreds of corpses scattered throughout the complex.

Nancy Wong's picture of Jim Jones

While the scene was apocalyptic, it is not clear that Jones had a theology clearly based on the Book of Revelation, unlike David Koresh, leader of the Branch Davidians. Koresh had deep convictions based on the Book of Daniel and the Book of Revelation, and his sect believed the world was in the power of Satan and that the nations were merging to form a new Babylon. David hoped to establish the kingdom in Jerusalem, where, according to him, he would suffer martyrdom. The headquarters of the sect was a complex called Mount Carmel Center located in Waco, Texas.

In 1993, the police received information that Koresh and his people were amassing high-powered weapons, and when they went to inspect, they were fired upon, which prompted the involvement of the federal government. After a 51-day long siege by federal agents, the FBI began a tear gas assault, and in the midst of the attack, Koresh called 911 to provide his last preaching, quoting from the Book of Revelation and mentioning the Seven Seals. The siege ended with the death of 75 persons, many of them women and children, as the Mount Carmel Complex burned to ashes in what was called a self-immolation ordered by Koresh.

Koresh

In the last manuscript produced by Koresh, which was preserved by a woman named Ruth Riddle who escaped the fire, the cult leader spoke extensively about his identity and the mystery of the Seven Seals. Koresh claimed to be the mysterious Lamb of Revelation who opens the sealed scroll, as well as the figure who rides the White Horse when the first seal is opened.

Four years later, another mass suicide conducted by another doomsday cult, Heaven's Gate located in San Diego, California, made headlines around the world. Although the cult did not speak in Christian terms, it was clearly apocalyptic, and its belief system was a strange mix between science fiction and the basic message of Revelation. The cult's leader, Marshall Applewhite, and his female companion, Bonnie Nettles, concluded that they were the two witnesses mentioned in Revelation 11:3-4: "And I will give power to my two witnesses, and they will prophesy one thousand two hundred and sixty days, clothed in sackcloth. These are the two olive trees and the two lampstands standing before the God of the Earth."

Applewhite believed the Earth would be transformed and renewed, and that evil entities (not beasts, but in this case, aliens) called Luciferans conspired against humanity. In his view, the elect members of Heaven's Gate would be taken up to a spaceship when the hour came. The opportunity to join the Rapture arrived with the passing of comet Hale-Bopp in 1997. Applewhite told his congregation that a spaceship was following the comet, and that the event would mark the closure of the gates of Heaven, making the spaceship the last opportunity to leave Earth. Over the course of three days, 38 members committed ritual mass suicide, all dressed identically, to be taken up by the UFO.

Influence on Modern Art

Like many of the New Testament texts, the origins of the Book of Revelation are shrouded in mystery. Since the 2nd century CE, the book has been the most disturbing and mysterious for Christians. Such is the continuing fascination with John´s visions that they still pervade in the entertainment industry, which has led to heavy metal records, blockbusters about the Rapture, novels about the end of the world, documentaries, and even political movements. Fundamentalists of every generation have thought the book was directed at them, and that the events it describes are happening in the present.

In the mid-1990s, the general public's fascination with Revelation was reawakened by the novel *Left Behind*, which, along with its 14 sequels, sold more than 65 million copies. The first novel begins with the Rapture, the climactic moment in time when thousands or millions of people literally disappear from Earth, those whom God has decided to preserve from the big fire. Those who stay on Earth, the ones left behind, must face what comes next, and the different installments explore the events leading to the great final battle between the divine and evil forces. The series has been criticized for its anti-Catholic and anti-Jewish views alike. Like many ultra-conservative radical Christians in Washington, the *Left Behind* series promoted the belief that the end of the world will begin with a powerful and self-sufficient Israel as a prerequisite for Christ's return. This means supporting Israel is a must, although not for the most honest reasons, because in the end, the Jews will have to convert or be annihilated.

Christianity, church attendance, and public trust in the clergy may be on the decline, but John the Revelator continues to enjoy enormous popularity. This is in part because people have found an explanation for the rise of powerful and menacing forces through his mighty metaphors, as well as the hope that one day they will be controlled and annihilated. The idea that a person, an Antichrist, or an institution is in charge of the world, and that modern socities are all its victims, are very attractive and simplifies things. Hence, an individual such as the president of the United States, Russia´s Vladimir Putin, or multi-billionaires such as Bill Gates or Mark Zuckerberg can be depicted as the terrifying being who through deception has put his mark on humanity, controls trade, and determines who lives or who dies, all while blinded people worship him as if he were a god: "And he causeth all, both small and great, rich and poor, free and bond, to receive a mark in their right hand or in their foreheads, that no man might buy or sell, save he that had the mark or the name of the beast or the number of his name." (Revelation 13:16-17).

The popularity of the apocalypse has been reignited not only by the turn of the millennium in 1999, but also the fall of the World Trade Center in 2001 and the coronavirus pandemic in 2020. This is something that is repeated and predictably will continue to be repeated in each generation.

Through it all, the book written almost two thousand years ago by a previously unknown prophet from Asia Minor named John continues to attract the interest, fascination, and fear of people across the world. For however long the world lasts, the Book of Revelation, with its fantastic cast of beasts, angels, riders, dragons, and divine avengers, is likely to last with it.

Online Resources

Other books about Christianity by Charles River Editors

Other books about the Book of Revelation on Amazon

Bibliography

Bauckham, Richard. *The Climax of Prophecy: Studies on the Book of Revelation.* T & T Clark, 1993.

Kirsch, Jonathan. *A History of the End of The World.* Harper Collins, 2006.

Leonard, Robert. *Visions of Apocalypse. What Jews, Christians, and Muslims Believe about the End Times, and How Those Beliefs Affect Our World.* National Security Analysis Department of The Johns Hopkins University Applied Physics Laboratory, 2010.

Pagels, Elaine. *Revelations: Visions, Prophecy & Politics in the Book of Revelation.* Penguin, 2012.

Thompson, Leonard L. *The Book of Revelation: Apocalypse and Empire.* Oxford University Press, 1990.

Yarbro Collins, Adela. *Crisis and Catharsis: The Power of the Apocalypse.* The Westminster Press, 1993.

Free Books by Charles River Editors

We have brand new titles available for free most days of the week. To see which of our titles are currently free, click on this link.

Discounted Books by Charles River Editors

We have titles at a discount price of just 99 cents everyday. To see which of our titles are currently 99 cents, click on this link.

Made in the USA
Columbia, SC
30 March 2026